Conundrums of Indignant Bliss

D.J. Haliday

Poetry Attic Press

Minneapolis

2019

Copyright © 2019 by D.J. Haliday.

All rights reserved.

Library of Congress
Cataloging in Publication Data

ISBN 978-0-9847218-2-5
First Printing 2019.

For information contact
www.poetryattic.com

Contents

1   Declining Influence of Us
2   Terminal Bar
6   Says the Man to The Setting Sun
8   Hamlet
11   We Love and Take for Granted All The Time
13   Runway Lights
15   Finite Injustice
18   The Littleness of Our Bigness
21   Of The Whispering
24   The Smell of Polynesian Capital
28   Out of Sync
30   Easy Loving
33   Unmistakable Signs of Decline
35   Shedding Skin
36   We Are Undefined
41   The Genius That Must
42   The Empire Builder
55   Parentage
57   Down River
61   The Festering
63   Anger Phase
64   Shadows of Death
73   Glass Hockey Stick
74   The Indiscretion of Solitude
80   Twilight
81   Limboland

Possible loves are for fools
Wise men feel impossible loves

- Spanish Proverb

Declining Influence of Us

Crushing mass, towering
over the entropy of progress.
Great swirling seas overflowing,
languid and percussive, shaking snow off a
still frozen morning.
Western mind before the Buddha,
cocky and humble, a spirituality of arrogance,
challenging
the simplicity of conformity,
                             as aliens storm the gate,
wary of love at a distance, wondering of fools to adore
for a better tomorrow, eager
to unlearn, absorb and grow.

Limited but by our own imprisonment,
Innocent, in our cynical awareness of yesterday,
praying
to Earth and all her deities for miracles
to forestall impending truth.

Terminal Bar

I've been around the world since last I've been here,
You all look the same, but so much has changed.

This beer tastes so much better than before,
for I've been stuck in the ditch, frustrated, angry
swearing my head off and freezing my soul
on an old engine seems it won't start again,

picked apart by vultures,
armchair critics, foes and
friends who seem to have
lost the art of folly.

Awoken,
in nightmares of will stranded
by endless news of defeat, while the omnipotent
beat of war doesn't cease, I wonder

    How can we be the monsters in the shadows?

I've been captured in a rank and file line,
having to salute to avoid getting shot
while cavorting with witches, debutants and saints
who've sent my soul and body spinning
painfully in delightful enchantment.

Hurled out of my flesh, I retreated to depths
where I've had to face myself alone
in dark caverns of the helpless void
where convenient rope ladders of mediocrity
will not do,

  where no faint light of hope is enough
  to sustain the withering buds
  of innocence and youth.

It was here I had to cross the line
to usher in new life, shuddering in
fear and awkward, blinding hatred

for soldiers stampeding their own promised heaven,
 far from bliss of dew, close to hunger growling.
Revulsion how far
from enduring
 solutions, sanity or understanding?

Ravaging Earth with terror, displacing
babies, families and lovers, born and unborn,
generations will come, bludgeoning
      life, spilling blood for Earth's oil,

expensing forests for concrete, air and water for raping
life's force raging, fracked, feverishly heating, oceans
choking,
her drying crust quakes,

While small and mighty minds delight
  in throwing stones to protect thrones,
  squinting from mirrors reflecting the
  inner light of our own short sight.

There cannot be a war on terror
  when the ultimate terror is war,
Nor does hatred grow from a void.

Innocent, we are born seeking love,
  warm affection and tender coddling,

Before our love becomes feared through slogans
on the street, perceptions ill-conceived,
imagination hammered into paths of least resistance,
convenient retreats of material seclusion as tears dry
from sacrificing years gone by
while the big clock of human destiny ticks
in sync with our mortal heartbeats,
violently seeking peace, spitefully loving,
struggling to find light and potency to not
hate or act in a manner in which the means
contradict the aim.

Sedulously growing an independent shuffle,
entwined with the dew of possible passion,
horizons we may never cross but must always keep alive,
for futures we will never know, dependent
on our hours.

I've been more discerning of these alleyways,
challenging, not relinquishing, tough, unrewarded love,
tingling and aching, feverishly aglow. I feel I've been
around the world one hundred times
since last I've been here with you, and calm
is my soul.

I'm ready now, to embrace my imperfect mortality,
seize this vital season in our history without
stampeding to the next, ignoring its effects,
smelling plastic roses, fearing a phantom enemy.

Will jaded hearts reawaken
from schemes of accepted deceit
      and routines of deathful living?

In those caverns of the helpless void, I've seen a grim face
stand between pride and a smile of grace,
in mirrors others help compose but cannot cross.

Shall we turn inside ourselves
to wring the fear and hatred out, forgive
the past and try again, to glimpse,
convey and realize the dawn?

And like a cocoon from which tender wings evolve,
let this soulful night fade on.

Says The Man To The Setting Sun

Says the man to the setting sun, "Beware of delicious pleasures sucking your soul, retouching images of adolescent gold to make dubious claims on righteousness and truth."

Achoo!

Sneezing slippers of pea pods & granules, Kodachrome rice fields, minuet landscapes, interruptions from daydreams to born again banquets aligned with an unconfiscated, karmic shroud.

Says the setting sun to the man, "Don't forget the people of Afghanistan who, gilded by the coming of a darker age, have neither want nor need of Western interrogation."

Says the moon to the receiver, taken hostage by a dreamy skateboard, shot at by benevolence and shaken with a twist of cunning opulence, "Silence warranties the best teacher."

While down home they do it real
not virtual, tread not steel, no free
white privileged parts for sale, no
trophies for drama or sympathy for
the devil,

Organic, in the muddy foundation of cotton fields,
intricacies of questionable worth sink the jetty,
rock operas for dummies, spies on satellite
tiptoe

in the net worth of invisibility.

Hamlet

Digging high
 heels in the road, gallantly living
off history's foes, precariously dwelling
    on idleness within
        as bureaucracy tames
the shrewdest of crews,
                halfway to heaven or Timbuktu,

A pilgrim's mission trivialized,
irrelevant but to an internal, far off vision.

Dispositions from the war
make it hard to sustain a façade of happiness.

The Dream dissolves and seeps
        eerily towards a blood-soaked reminder
 of the fallacy of innocence.

Imperfections undisclosed, provoked reprisals,
banks loaning robbers reaping golden sands,
sacred lands defiled for tourists, a ribbon cutting
ceremony blown by spirit winds, limbs torn and
scattered, bulldozed, and caught on cameras, gone
viral, leaving children alone and crying, seas
swelling in calm vacation sun, best intentions
ruined, loved ones lost.

Favor and texture abandoned, heads down.
Instead of merry rye, cry broken angels
In cynical regression, odes to occupying
soldiers beneath heavy skies of bombastic
chatter - a wordless gasp, a nervous tear
splashing reality on the wall.

When suddenly,
strained relations become an uneasy truce
while orders come and seldom go
to crush the volatile dynamo,
forestalling possibilities, dangling fear
as short sight is a short cut to lead
the status quo.

What's it all for? Living by a
fence post guarding borders,

What do I know? Sheltered in a cobweb, caught
hanging on a heckled view, gobbling
resources, contributing little to the stew.

I've had it all - tonsillitis and chicken pox, cocktails
in first class, been high on snowcapped vistas,
breathing deep in colorful reefs, no less underwater
than the rest. I've danced with buoyed dignity, sulked
with indignant pride, bargaining with the reaper for
another ride on the Empire Builder in November
with an iPod, two beers and a native interpreter
to confuse the question of who belongs where.

Impounded with decibels of deafening silence
sacrificed for suntanned news wired from somewhere,
beyond absurdity stains on the killing room floor,
hoodwinks and balderdash, rare bits of sanity
cured into brisket, aged on divorce.

Heaven turns its back on an advantageous past,
fusing the journey with blinded steps
while the future creeps unvarnished.

Eighty-six
million barrels every
day in exchange
for glaciers

dwindling. Majority, where

is the fine boundary to heaven
vanquished by indiscriminate
believers fooled into thinking
that we cannot all be rich?

We Love and Take for Granted All The Time

We love and take for granted all the time
those things that are yours and things that are mine.

Were it any other time, I could see fit to fly
with you on through this splendid day, strewn
with bright hues of orange and gold
to fortify us
against the coming cold.

Were it something new to behold,
would it matter any deeper
than a new apprehension of silhouettes
against a dimming sky?

Tall blowing grasses, freely eternal,
locked in time,

warm youthful hope, please never
leave my mind.

Smiles across fields of endless possibilities of love,
before the rushing tide comes in, before
the break wall cracks.

We've a new world now.
Nostalgia reformats a republican march.
Never quite irrelevant, seldom as appropriate

as hanging out in a record store
in Winona or Kolkata, discovering grooves of new
seeds of passion. Fighting off cynicism,

waking
in echoing halls amidst the walls we
bashed our heads against,

nightmares of embarrassments nagging.
Walls just made by people after all.

The love we take for granted still divine,
if only we could be there at the time.

Is this surface petty? Are you thrown now for a loop?
Can we glimpse beyond our mirrors to grow and give?

Was I? And whom now are you?

Ornament at my side, playing the puppet strings.
Short years, guarded smiles, long silence of dignity.

Accomplishments wearing humility
as love deepens, bold as the afternoon.

Runway Lights

One last call to make from the tarmac:
  How do we get that message across?
  What do we communicate? Where
    do we go from here?

Wheels up and off,
a thousand miles tossed
to remembrance and anticipation.

Time flies away from runway lights
through open fields, towards a cliff,
over the edge, up into the mist, chasing
away antiquities and resistance.

Riding home
to fading claims to empire.
Democracy let Barnum Bailey run the circus,
turning nightmares to commodities, brilliantly
portrayed

rhetoric so old and effective,
        powerful plots to fuel a war,
medieval beheadings as modern cameras roll,
reclaimed by oceans as we lose out owning
anomalies evolving.

Strange how the last ten went by like a whim,
racing towards that summit of meticulous goals
to slalom into paradise, obscured beneath
high blue heavens.

Navigating by the glow of laptop light,
movies and spreadsheets, digital dreams -
Call it freedom. Call it peace.
Tarnished flagpole, garnished wage, virtual
wisdom confronted

as a big machine,
maybe an airplane, maybe a heart,

boldly descends
through clouded reconciliation.

Finite Injustice

I think of the computational bore
whose work we all adore, befitting
future citizenry

while a group of allies
intently listens to confusing refutations
of known order, increasing speculation
of heavy, tattered baggage that frankly
needs to go,

stains sucking up the limelight,
a cluster of pride for the uninitiated, taking
gains and losses all in stride.

I think of that once mighty woman,
her debonair charm and sexual prowess, her choice
of refinement over those reckless
male moves,

now stuck and placed conveniently
upon a higher pedestal and lower shelf,
bleeding burdens of mortality's suckling
for life and family, tossed to make way
for gears of progress, grinding humanity
into a sexless aloofness, bundled
with astute difference.

It's not about
the folly of romance,
but a much longer dance to the grave,

she masters fiercely,
atoning for wages discounted
and taken for granted attitudes
towards superlative guesses.

I think of the ancestors
who never received medals but shackles,
whose history has always been discounted

like the Natives and the Land,
overlooked by the innocent offspring
of conquerors, unwilling to question
the moral reasoning of equality.

And who should spy the dignified
by deeper stalking of the stripes?

Cloaked and unacknowledged,
too horrible to comprehend,
too detrimental to success,

At best, the conquest pauses,
acknowledging debt, before
continuing unabated.

There's little ammo in a cup of decency
for the short run.

In the deepening cosmos
do our acknowledgments deliver

true freedom
from the tyranny of yesteryear.

The Littleness of Our Bigness

The bigness of our littleness,
prism of myriads, strength in numbers,
oneness of our fractured shards,

eager chatter, tit for tat, otter and rat.

Fraternizing enemies within
foes of soul hid outside the matrix,
loose screws rattling glass ceilings.
projected through innocent others -
counterpoints, lovers and other
disassociates, wielding
their own baggage to the slough,

It's a wonder airplanes don't crash, highways
turn to wreckage more often as the bigness
of our littleness scatters effervescently into
notions of sacredness and cynicism,

Like witty revelations of dumbstruck reckoning,
cosmic observations of misaligned reasoning
dance round a pole,

trendy and dated, eternally enrolled
as the littleness of our bigness unfolds

in blood splotches in the news and toilet bowl,
in the demise and hope for our children,
in the snide bickering line drawn across the house,
 A cold civil war

distracted by smartphones
and wisecracking sneers,
hogging bandwidth for
immediate twitter,

Core resources towards electric
cheers for fear, impenetrable stability
of Manhattan not withstanding

insects biting guests in bed,
a covertly American grip on democracy,
uncompromising, dogmatic,
beacons of irrationality
belligerently facing away
from the hurricane,

Locking the pearly gates to the foreign
and ungreedy, sewing seeds of terror,
squandering futures for yesterdays,
tomorrows for moments.
Heaven rides on a shore of remorse
against penetrable tides of irrelevance
shied away from and ignored,

too paralyzing to contemplate
to merit its activity.

Salvation, a deceit away
from the bigness of our littleness,
bludgeoned by the littleness
of our bigness

in contradictions recognized and constipated
by liberal truths, conservative abortions and
rebirth, closeted vices torched by crowds of
lesser virtue,

human rights recloaked in freedom
granted for a hoax, Hollywood endings,
narcotic placebos, spiritual drain
on the dynamo

as progress builds a dam, floods the village,
stomping out their language altogether in a
rabid competition for diminishing space,
air, water, land, food and culture.

Shrine smashed. Temple mocked.
Samaritans load big guns for the walk.
Lessons lost. Survival found. Weak
links in the armor aroused.

The bigness of our littleness bows
before today's private moments
between lovers and associates,
paper armies, us and them,

in varying pigments of skin
and genetics, dress and culture,
ambitions and truths, irrelevant
but to ourselves, gasping

our last breath alone, surmising
the littleness of our bigness.

Of The Whispering

Sometimes living's hard.
Don't wanna wake from the
grace of a dream, crawl from
a warm bed out on the cold
floor of a November morn
to chores that'll tire 'til night.

Where goes love's light?

Sometimes living hurts.
Stains from the past still
hunt new horizons, seeding
stern clouds over easy days,
perhaps knowing that all
won't be right in the end
and there's nothing to living
but just getting on,

past those who've died, whose
embrace has now cooled.
Beyond the promise of exuberant smiles,
flesh starts to wrinkle,
hair, like life, thins,
aged souls harden, bleeding
whispered confessions of weighted
grasping.

Too paralyzed to conjure
up what next to do, I drink a Summit,
recalling barefoot surfing on a
fleeting summer breeze, intoxicated
by a magnificently gentle fragrance
of lilies enchanting the shade.

Petals shed like stardust from
forgotten skies, precious to the touch
as I succumb to the feast,

                              deep peace,
                                      unblemished,
                                appreciative,

          silent.

               Was I once full of unmitigated hope and light?

Destitute, on a prodding cloud,
hyperventilating clogged arteries
and hours, highways and bypasses,
brochured adventures for lost
connections, itinerate holiday
disfigured, undisturbed, away
from the destiny of reality.

Journeyed, met and grown, all flavors
of character and logic, epic scenes and
magic dreams, pretentiousness & insatiability,

and now

in keen tranquility,

    I revive

        that sense

            of sacredness,

                of self, of place,

            empathy, destiny,

      true spirituality.

The Smell of Polynesian Capital

Once I was a beatnik,
and in the grand tradition of great beatniks,
I, in forests uncharted, wandered

no clear path to nightfall
in the great foreplay of everyday.
Lightning striking, breaking images
into inline blisters, all adding up to
nothing much
but love.

Now the smell of Polynesian capital,
frankly, on a Bohemian dawn
of sacred grooves over stiff
       whiskey and cappuccinos
         beneath cigarette clouds
is dizzying among
bamboo.

Beer soaked streets stripped
      of innuendoes, barking suits and movie sets,
 stir in the directionless laid back sobriety
of Beat otherworldliness

Open
after closing time
to chat about Afghanistan.

Guns and capital in place of infrastructure,
maddening delight of recklessness relate
purpose to a stupor of identity.

Trust misplaced in a middle class séance,
brown haze and laugh tracks out of sync
with the Sensei,

necessities deactivated. Asian whirl of a girl in skinny
jeans taps into the muse where middle age goatees just
twist *"Obama or Karzai - Who would want to be
president?"*

Juju guitar cries like Charlie Parker among wind tossed
Chinese lanterns renewing the capacity for fate and folly,
opportunities and setbacks. Zoot suit riot or grapefruit
diet? Mix the two maniacally for a stale-free sunrise
routed towards that inner state of tumultuously
unstraightened affairs frozen in hot light of loneliness
surrounded by strangers familiar
with déjà vu indigestion, wondering,
Oh! Where has significance gone? Buoyed by
betrayed delusions, surviving beyond the sneer
of ego's dogma, pampers and shaving cream, Rice-a-
Roni in a jar, a magician's smokescreen,
velvet top hat tipped to a magic afternoon on Haight.

I can't surrender the cosmos,
nor San Francisco absurdity,
assistant in lace more lovely
than the magic,

Italy, where the sea

        whispers off heavy

                experience,

    it's metaphor strongly whirling
    ominous to China and Japan, not
    knowing when to quit, hit on or
    begin in the interim.

Sneakers hiking up Nob Hill
with pencils and notebook, sweet reefer waffling
through the street, indiscrete and luscious,
steeper than hopefuls dining on delivery,
vaguely rendering salient tomorrows puked
up for scents of love in a porcelain toilet hugged.

Purple shag, narrow plaid, and the smoke, I'm
telling you, *those cigarettes!*
Baguettes plump, bumping timid smiles into alleyways
to rendezvous with late night ferocity
before the heartbreak of cirrhosis hounds
purists of future ages endowed
with friendlier integrity than tourists,
who love to play the bongos barefoot, long hair waving
in the breeze
        living to dance,

                dancing to live.

                                    While,
                    I'll be forever
                    workin' til my dying day,

         coughed up by the past,
         crashed on the rocks,

   left for dead,

         hounded
           by dried blisters,

      It's all so fleeting.

But,
for a moment or thirty, I felt such happiness
wandering into Spec Adler's on a Monday night, like
twenty-five fucking years after first discovering
postcards on the bar,

feeling such satisfaction, such
spartan vagrancy of certainty,
such warmth inside, facing
the humbled compromise
of tomorrow's goat

as perhaps
a winning
after all.

Out of Sync

Could it be that everyone doesn't love a rock'n roller?
Would my neighbors rather church bells than the Dead
      on Sunday morn?

Could my religion incite fear and hatred
 in the minds of others oriented East
 instead of West? Right instead of Left?

Could my skin make me an enemy?
 My neighbors hold me in contempt?

What are these playing fields but different ends under
 the same blue sky? Morphed together
 by multi-national factories and kennels,
 compacting boundaries of age, sex and race,
 identity and ideology, Ferguson and Sandy Hook,
        Guantanamo and Abu Ghraib, Tibet
 and China, Palestine, news between the supplements
     advertising Mother's Day and father's pay.

Could it be that some don't comprehend the beauty
 in jubilant late night drinking into heavy mornings?

Impatiently floating for solid ground
 in ice cold glacial waters, Ursus Maritimus plunges
 adrift.

Could it be that entertainment is not an arbor
to hang out the damp rags of a diseased democracy
for exclusionist dissection or organic plea,
symbiotically retrieved by an ailing deity within?

Infidels with a grin, meat-eating gardeners
tabling a prescribed heaven, grafting
others to come to the manner, suited
by sustained pathways reigning.

Is my conduct a substantial factor in causing harm,
unproductive to life with more of it coming?

Deft of a thistle with a lime for the haze,
less left to graze, satin calls the knave
taking hold of the mold for a backbreaking load
on the crest of a billowing reason.

Hell holds together like glue
on a tightly-packed, carbon
belching freeway,

communicating through towers
worldwide, amplified,
virtually, virally.

Could it be that
my agony and bliss
isn't synching
with yours?

Easy Loving

I paid the price
for easy loving.

Paid a price
for all I've had.

Nothing came free,

> (Except for a mountain
>   of free, imported beer left
>   on the side of a Colorado
>   highway, a gift from God!
> Cold beer afloat in glacial
>   water swishing in a cooler across
>   the great divide between youth
>   and middle age).

Nothing came free,

Dreams nor wisdom,
heart nor mind,

Soul evolution,
I paid that price.

Some say the river dries, ozone thins,
globe warms, woman scorns, body aches,
love escapes, form pirate ways from ease
and poetry - I added to that mayhem.
I paid

for freedom's days blown lost and stranded
on missed breezes, foundationless,

Bohemian brilliance bulldozed
by hospital mornings broke and penniless,
balls hurting, body aching, soul bloviated
by routines hypnotized, blunders realized,
grown as heavy tumors,

Where Love stands sanitizing
the claiming of the prize,
looming long after the magic subsides,
ruling hard on possibilities
against the pragmatism of hours.

Afternoon's industrious capture
walks idyllic across adverse shores,

Timid adjustments to the grand machinery,
oiling sockets and watering sprouts,
washing faded jeans and hanging out,
lurking for a return path to significant clout.

Daydreaming of ice cream enchantment,

waning on a skating moon.

Heart still beating long after the ruin,

old enough to understand

and be here still

flirting with

you.

Unmistakable Signs of Decline

Losing altitude
losing market share
losing sanity and socks
losing ability to appreciate
comprehend and reciprocate
facilitate and masturbate
losing a rusty old river artifact
caught on a hook, indecent yet
respected, sentimental in a twisted
sort of way, aloof and altogether
fearful of repercussions and
consequences powerfully illogical
devastatingly delicious
death and over the hill irrelevance
losing respect and keen perspective
séance of humor and a craving to dance
new dimensions in a kiss
the calling of mischief from an alley
losing hair and muscle tone
memories and contact
passion and dimensions
all those things
traveling rough roads
through dawns sacrificed
for elevator music
for fuses blowing
tempers flaring
401k fading

ladle burning
entitlement embezzled
mischief and mayhem
to blame others for
sacrificing cousins
selfishly familiar
devilishly arresting
handcuffs of golden
injustice, life mortgaged
for a parking space, collateral
damage for a credit increase
manufactured piece
code conforming soul
turned to oil
in the soil.

Shedding Skin

Shedding layers
of misperceptions, conventions
and memories
conveniently molded into.

Hiding with pride,
adorned, remote,
now removed

to face again
an inalienable truth.

Fleshed out organs and bones,
unfeigned significance,

wield remains of
universal acuteness

addressed
to an unordered
hour.

We Are Undefined

  We are undefined, moving
    beyond ancient fights
      with our new songs.
        Our differences shared
          openly retrieving
            ourselves
        from our own exclusivity

  to a destiny
completely fresh,
      open, welcomed.

We are undefined,
          formless, nameless,
       bodies in an elevator
going up and down, not talking, not
        wincing, just gazing
     at the floor until the door
stops
    on our level.

And forward
       without questioning, we move,
unsure of ourselves but not
          letting it show,

Boldly,
    letting definitions of ourselves be determined
so it will be easier for us to find ourselves
     amidst a well known dimension.

Yet all of it may be wrong
        as we are undefined, capable
    of reinventing ourselves at any time, at any moment,
                    on any whim.

        Is it love or duty that ensnares us?
        The weight of law or weariness?

Species too destined to live,
        devolve
            humbly abridged.

Short excesses in a long haul,
        inequity mixes violent
            in the night.

Glacier calves in the early
        spring sun.
    Vesuvius burps on
            the cosmos.

  We do what we can to define ourselves
      and we go down together.

Young men off to join the jihad.
Ideals worth dying for.
A vision hard on the widowed heart,
suffering verbose shame and prejudice
while slave to a mortgage, victim of the
workweek, relentlessly mistrusted.

What mutual aim binds us?
What human jewel unique unites?
Why the façades and entropy dividing
     ancient injustice with biblical violence?

     We all do what we do.
        Taxi driver rambles against
  selfies with little ethos,
unsparing of nature,
    fallaciously entitled
        to foreign inspiration
                    for the taking.
Is what's yours
and what's mine
how we are defined?

Foolish humans wreaking peace,
    cause for police,
        vipers for stardom.

Leadership drains with dwindled respect.
Order maintained at the cost of compassion,
lacking an arsenal of superpower virtue as
a bellwether trial of indignant prosperity
saddles worlds won and lost.

    We all do go down together
        pulled around, pushed
   by the whipping wind
upon a dog-eared eyeball,
    heart pounding,

bliss lost and won on shoulders
                    of giants and fools.

  History composed with blood on our hands,
  seduced by skin color and the sins
  of shallow entrenchment by fore founders.

        We enter
                to re-envision
                    our world,
                to stand
                        shoulder to shoulder
                            abiding.
We must
    stop the hatred,
            halt the fear,
        the unknowing,
            misunderstanding,

                    Jump start hope
                    for tomorrows
                        for all the living,
                                regardless
    of breed and creeds,
        institutions and notions divisive

for all entities of earth
to speak
understanding

of our world
too precious

to violently bicker
with
weapons of destruction

which are not
tools for building
hope, only apocalyptic
terror,
unlove,
human implosion,

overproducing, cannibalizing
rapidly devolving, all for a
small ripple in the universe.

With ourselves, with each other, We
must
all
make
peace.

The Genius That Must

The genius that was
is the genius that is

but must be done now
or never will be.

The genius that is
is the genius that was

undisguised,
recognizable

by indifferent acceptance
of a tune immune
to process.

Angry seas flood the gallows
brilliantly relevant, poetically demure.

The genius that was
is the genius that is

but must be done now
or never will be.

The Empire Builder

I.

The movers and shakers don't sleep.
Movement consumes their lifeblood.
Their hearts beat restless, unfulfilled,
propelled by purpose, caffeine and Red Bull,
necessity and driven needs, spiritual and material,

to compensate losses of bruised childhoods
and bad marriages, polio and missing limbs,
community hunger and stinging failures.
What drives humankind is not bliss.

They say if the weather in Germany
was as fine as in Greece, the trains
wouldn't run on time either.

They say a starving fool is eager, but
 who are they espousing pop wisdom
 in favor of their own limitations?

Quivering in the cold darkness of our
last foundation, laid to rest in weary
bonds by misunderstood lovers
for decency and convenience sake,

Is comfort all love really is after all?

Moments of delusion follow acceptance,
replacing dreams that once drove,

We've a long way to go.

II.

Riding smooth iron rails across the country
through a cool Montana night, effortless,
except for the fossils pumped, except for
a hierarchy of unacknowledged debt, an
anarchy of vision, complete with no remorse
or forgiveness. Tenderness and history abandoned,
interwoven with the smell of shit and piss,
cigarettes, gasoline & sulfur, burning air and flesh,

Come ride this train with me, my friends,
come ride the train with me,
through tonight's black velvet veil
on this steadfast, midnight rail

into gravitational fog of hidden certainty,
traversing icy bridges of discretion and indifference,
rails of decrepit insidiousness veiled by meddling
madmen, occupied lovers and intermediary bureaucrats
all putting in a day's work for a day's pay and getting
no further than the next stop at Minot.

The clickety-clack of these cross-country tracks
circumvented by complementing chatter,
Disneyland facts, potpies and cheesecake,
despite convections of the media sitter,
Auschwitz and Iraq, Syria and Standing Rock,
offer a comfortable retreat from a journey unhinged.

Wolf Point, Great Bend, Le Havre

Real men don't quiver
with guilt for acquitted rapes and famed conquests
but stand tall on the shoulders of giants
over endless generations and cultures
defending Goddess, God and Country,
        twisting tremendously the fabric.

A tearing sense of decency plows
across more foreign fields, grazing, taking
in an almighty vanquishment of unredeemable greed,
forever grasping,
killing for love, respect and worth,
deceiving ourselves of our righteousness
that Natives were slain for
 and the Slave's blood was traded for.

A mother endures as child beholds with angry fists.

Slaves to the auction, witches to the stake,
war on the tele, market strewn with blood,
drowned by griping in the club car about the price
of gas at pumps. Damn foreigners aren't
we all, ungrateful protestors the lot of us.

Arthritic fingers, heart attack survivor with
a weakened liver rises, spitting as he shouts
 *"You want me to taste the bitterness of
  hatred, blood, & guts?"*

As young fingers learn new chords on a big guitar
playing to the moving whistle of the Empire Builder,

> *Come ride this train with me, my friends*
> *Sleep, with me*
> *In my dreams*
> *Be with me*
> *In my tormented nightmares*
> *In the color of my skin, the gravity of my brain*
> *The amplification of my voice*
> *So I can be here with you.*

III.

I've mellowed now, I've been struck down.
Many matchbooks struck and tossed
and I'm no further than my counter facing
neighbor, just another passenger getting on,
stalked by inambition and failing humor,
worn gray by roles of breadwinning and
parenthood, still wondering, as my perspective
ages, Is humanity rich or poor? What is freedom?
A bullet in the market on your son's birthday?
A right to lesser schools, roads and public services?

Instead of being angry, I want to give thanks
for life too valuable for cannon fodder,
for breath to aid solutions,
to seed the world more peacefully with arms
for embracing not obliteration.

Growing in a crowding berth, filling up
with eighty million more per year, faster
than the Dow Jones on a planet of seven billion where
obesity competes with hunger, species vanish, opposing
creeds of peace fight each other for forests receding as
seas rise; the strongest survive this ubiquitous tide.

Looking round the bend to catch a view
towards deeds outpacing carnage,
the decency of humility, potential of humanity,

                                              Or am I so off,

Lost in towering edifices atop metropolis,
born on the trail of the western white man
through cold Montana snow, iridescent
as it reflects a lonely winter moon?

Ragged flag flapping in a fierce night
for fresh dead coming home with honors
hidden from the camera's view.

IV.

Mother was unarmed. The soldier fired first.
When the missile fell, the party ended.
No more groom. No more bride.
No more in-laws from which to hide.
Happily ever after.

Suddenly the car is silent as a cargo hold, stripped
of time and substance, possibility and hours devoted
to the true, deep, sensuous pleasure of laughing
at the cosmic, desperate grandeur of it all.

Mirrors in the ceiling reflect queer attacks on the pier.
Jazzier than accountant lunches, Samaritans turn back.

No prison scuffles, called it in,
     guiding the warheads to change quick the tune,
premiering
     captivating, in-flight action movies with windows
closed to dim the outside light,
     where few gaze deeply towards the veiled
blood staining victims
     counted as enemies - mothers and bakers and
aunties and sons
          enticing combatants more numerous
than generations can overcome.

Storm clouds herd above iron tracks of certainty
        shaking the earth.
Had a dream I was a black man hating white men, a
        brown man hating black men, a Hindu hating
                Muslims, a Jew hating Palestinians,
as I tried to parse whose hatred is justified? Whose
violence constructs? Whose end justifies the means?
Who can harness their emotions to better shape a just
landscape?

Lately the suckers have all gone to bat
mocking the hustlers while arming a coup,
while a man in the big suit says he's
ridding a tyrant, killing, in the process,
far more than his foe, wiping out
compassion with the upper hand of terror.
Child cries foul of the whole damn dance
on a violent street outside, a barbed wire
barricaded precinct station to protect
and serve, as the train rolls by.

Club car folk mock this tinted news on tv,
don't care much for history, seldom look
under the hood to examine the holdup, noting
only angrily the inconvenience on their way to the
station.

V.

Are we all born equal? Is opportunity a privilege or a
 right?
The left points fingers at the right. East lobs insults at the
 West.
Both white and black suppress the browns while the
 existing discredit the alien and unborn.

All of it hurts
and none of it works.
The chaos feeds the clickety-clack,
strengthening a martinet dispelling rumors that
A people
Divided
Will never be
United.

It makes no sense, this foreign mess,
A language of covered, unknown heads.
Can I stand for you and you for me?
Embrace our difference to rectify
the inequity of justice raging in the dining car?
Is democracy a fallacy? A failed dream?
This for you and that for me,
blind eyes towards eternity.
Isn't nature enough violence
after all?

VI.

We've a long way to go, rerouted
by short term destinations, obedient passions,
the douchebagification of a generation hungover
from yesterday's marginalized critique of personal
deceit,

> *Come ride*
>   *these rails*
>   *with me*
>   *my friends*
>   *Come ride*
>   *these rails*
>
>   *with me*
>   *to witness*

Ghost dancers barefoot in the blizzard,
huddled in blankets of smallpox, starving,
cotton shacks and rivers of fire, tight-lipped
Manzanar and Baltimore, armies for the ire,
disappearing seasons, South regrets the North,
old despise the young, short men hate the
tall man, abused woman spurns all men,
blessings of Earth eclipsed
by demons made with iron fists.

We've a long war to throw,
many seeds to sew. We
can't escape, have to relate.

Fire up some baseball and loosen the rates,
skewer the obnoxious by fostering debate.
Division among brothers ain't nothing new,
but jeez, how're we gonna create something lasting
among these ruins of humanity's gaffes?

Honey, who's driving this train?

Making war to make peace,
building walls for hate to cease,
using banners of religion and democracy
as cloaks for greed and tyranny
with lots of goodies offered up
to keep we people all checked out
in lullabies of our righteousness so as
not to stir our souls with the blood spent
in human embarrassments unkind
shed for remains of the absent
spirits deadened before life's end,
seems to me we're all to blame,

Honey, who's holding the reigns?

Cough up the mustard, stop babying the mare,
freedom dwindles in eyes of the scared,
Wary vibrations from a shrinking world call,
outweighing the oppressor, imprisoned by coupons,
Watching ruin progress in high definition
tightly produced with spectacular vision.

Zombies and villains, obsessed
with grand weapons, vex
a real unaccomplished toast,
red eyed to another coast, racing
sunset's riling hours
 into a conniption fit of orange

rage blighted in denial as the atmosphere degenerates
to fear and misaligned indignation. Glaciers calve
into rising seas sinking great cities, drowning breasts.
Resources vanquished to a weapon's cache. Storm
clouds roll to thunder, lumbering

over the iron and metal, passenger, tanker and boxcars
stampeding forthright through the storm as the midnight
locomotive chases its hole to the universe.

VII.

Lightening exposes a barren horizon
beyond rhythms of the train.

There's a hole in the ice where compassion lingers,
where snarling dogs quench their thirst
tending the local while the global writhes
one hemisphere over another.

Expectations put to a test
of fanciful dreams awakened suddenly
to a challenged foundation of easy truths flawed,
stealing tomorrows from yesterday,
cracking the veneer of a mighty powder keg,
aging bewildered by intelligible design
as flames engulf the parachutes,
Fracked landscape quakes and poison seeps,
collapsing shock absorbers beneath the faults, jolting
passengers violently alert on suddenly uneven terrain,
upending hierarchy and guarded wisdom,
appropriation and racist keys,
tablecloth flapping in a fierce sudden breeze,
Armageddon takes the porcelain,
dashing hopes
of a long way to go.

        Gonna get there? I don't know.

Tie-dyed threads worn bare and faded,
nearsighted, encircling enterprises,
out of tune tripping on high voltage wires,
malfunctions of human distortion.
Such destruction.   Is human
evolution even possible?

VIII.

The horizon is just
a mirage of an accomplishment,
n'er to be taken for granted.

Red necks from leather straps. Oxen plowing.
Home thaws, heats.
A high price paid for the progress.

Proceeding with caution, administering
a painful divorce
from yesterday's prejudice upon today's reality.

Some say there's no fairness in nature anyway.
Retreating from the rising sea, I wonder
how vast the beauty in eternity we wander?

Riding smooth iron scars across a cold American night,
effortless, except for the coal pumped,
except for history travelled upon

      the weight of today's news
staining tomorrow,

our unacknowledged debt
to perishability.

Parentage

Sweet scent of succulent lovers
masquerading in yesterday's worn clothes,
Love in the grass, does it last?

Trifling in morning sun, full coat
under moist dew, lilies wide open,
benevolently vulnerable,

magnificently
offering fragrance to
intoxicate the morning gust.

Without retreating,
this beauty and the sunken treasure
are nearly motionless as a battlefield

Soon to be a graveyard overturned
by bulldozers, irrespective of the great personal
significance of this failed initiative.

Now the pretty diamonds have all come to pass.
Sparkle off the princess. Vivacity off the throne.
Home is a dust blown heap of disarray,

A hallway of commuters, to and fro rushing
while the thing in the basement grows
benign and malignant.

Experience damages an unbridled smile.
Worn grooves beneath an endless sky.
Lines on dry skin.

Efforts for the future
thwarted.
Battle lost.

It's all I can do to walk these sore
bones and hold my head in dignity,
betrayed by the closest to the cause.

Love in the grass, does it grow?
A child's kiss to really call home.
A laugh, a sigh.

A tourniquet to stop
the bleeding.

Downriver

Buggy, humid night
    Passing shores so close,
Reality left upriver
  Facing the long journey down.

Afforded a view of infinity's
Blutopia,
vibrantly heckled as the men
drink coffee, eat their beans.

 Where am I within this team?

Small fish in the stream, deckhand on a barge,
smug and penitent, affected, uncertain,
as literate prodding conflagrates.

Rat trap in a drain ditch, forwarding
communiqués of perilous merit
to an upturned nose of aristocracy beguiled
     by toothless incantations of expedient lineage.

A democratic image, painfully just, trying to loosen
the grip, fighting with remote fury, unhassled
but for the brindled bureaucracy of inward negotiation,
     petrified by inaction, losing daylight schemes
and access to gentling hues, a sense of
worthiness in some direction,
floating down.

Tainted towards the steeping stew,
guided by a robust stout, ain't nothing new,
its been this way for lifetimes now, just a
ripple in the effervescent unfolding of largeness
overshadowing devilish details of the cause,

Passionate, resilient, nobly focused
narrowly towards where
Old Man River meets the gulf.

The men engage banter and warfare
with women too, tangled up in
body fluids and isolation, fused
thrones and burdensome futures,
tending bones and organs
with affectionate irreverence,
attitudes and prejudice,
longing and compromise.

Whims of the river suck daylight,
dreams bludgeon easy convention,
hound respectable goals, making
bearded trolls of Target shoppers,
desperate divas foreign to a foothold,
fighting the haphazard nature of falling in line
where the team huddles and games are played
  a scant distance from more universal logic.

   The scent of a passing forest
      ceremoniously savored
     for a dance with the cosmos coming out
       to romance
          a truer circumstance.

While below deck
men drink coffee, eat the beans,
catch the meat, cook the stew,
nothing new.

Slow evolution.

If you wanna be starting something,
blessed be, give yourself up
to the universe drifting
indifferent, unpredictable.

No sense in not trying.

Glory eludes the undignified
seeking comfort in exhaustion,
concentration fractured by the bungling,
fighting for a name, a lone flag posted
to stand in an eternity of nothing much
but spitfire aloofness,

Trite ambition,
   a garden to tend
       in wake of the weight drifting down.

A penetrating hyperbole accompanies Dixieland,
safely entombed in a shining star, illuminating
the impossibility of perfection, contained by smiles
known,

shading unique features compromised,
bonding innuendoes and frayed footprints
towards replacement of identity

buried in a slough of reasoning,
faintly holding on
to promise and regret

as the river swells miraculously,
sweet rain brings another dawn,
deliciously underrated and dwarfed

by illusionary sonnets and
sharp, narrow focus, making
the familiar host a ghost

while roasting the exotic
and new on the
broken back of dedication.

The Festering

Show-stopping empty casings,
  discarding tainted blow,
      deprived man and contraband
      meet on a dead end street,

feigning indignation over fingerprints,
inked in the news, aired on TV,
aggravated by the suffering of villains
neither black nor white,
disproportionately identified.

It's tough to keep it all together.

You get pissed off, knocked down, set up,
on the defense instead of offering solutions,

angered by shallow analysis,
paralyzed by bruising fear,
misguided by violent drumbeats,

compassion starved, learning stunted,
dismal progress
towards a peaceful inheritance.

The festering pain of a community,
disjointed, abused so often
as to not accept
any narrative
except disbelief,

shoots fearful blind retaliation
from the hip, no attempt
to understand,
knowing how the system works,

trying only to diffuse the situation,
superciliously believing in the
permanence of foundations.

While the probability of surrender
always lurks,
waiting for a misstep to tempt
the easily entrusted and distracted.

Anger Phase

Could humanity recover
from its angry face?

To grow without violence?
Peace without war?

Riches buried beneath
bullshit, wrenched
in the gears
of great evolution.

Both sides of the aisle
bogged down in a history
of preventing future embraces,

glorifying infinite growth
as possible,

falsely behind the hidden grimace
of centuries of oppression

doubtful to recover from
her angry face.

Shadows of Death

I.

Shortly after Angelina died,
she dropped by unexpectedly
to remind me of what it was
to be in love,

that inspired, sacred feeling,
effervescent and indestructible.

She didn't return to remind me of her cancer,
her pain, the failed dream and broken home,

only of love and the grand promise
to transform any landscape,
       inspiring the music that she had lost,

conjuring kingpins for monetary mastery
over admittance to the one percent,
her ornate lobby of opulence.

But even all of Steve Job's money
couldn't save his life,
Nor can the comforts of technology
guarantee love's survival.

Speeding privileged, hard working,
failing on a grand level that few even knew,
(most only envied while enduring limitations
of their age) surviving
in an allergy free balloon
with artificial limbs and only
determination and composure
lest it all be too late
as that beautiful smile succumbs
to mounting surgeries and failing relations,
paid for by the hardening ruthlessness
of self-preservation.

Angelina visited to reclaim all she
had lost in life, to erase the image
of who she was from her deathbed,
who she had become but not who
she was when she was young.

And I have to look away
as she drives off down the alley,

look away as Republics spin their scene,
look away as airplanes fall from the sky,
look away from another's nervous eye,
wondering
if we are all prisoners
of love, of greed, prisoners of TV,
credit cards and SUV's, prisoners
of doctrine, prisoners of art, the work,
the grind that grafts our souls, turns
mold to stone, earth to ash,

humble revolutions, for what they're worth,
spears and bullets, bombs and gas
prisoners of responsibility alas,

                        the values
that we share, arguments we wear, choices
we appraise, children that we raise, destiny
encumbers aisles walked in supermarket mazes,
surreal dikes protecting irreverent foundations,

an addiction counter of strange ambitions
    nagging on the radiated marrow, fidgeting
        in painfully bright hospital light,

I had to look away,

towards a soft candle flickering
in a room mostly void of furniture.

Long ago, a simple meal, a satisfying,
cheap bottle of wine,

taking for granted
that the future would be built
upon this hour of foreplay
    that proved instead to be
the crowning jewel.

II.

Driving North up Highway 61 from Winona
in early November, the brownness of the grass
swaying against forested shapes of feminine grandeur,

Left alone in frozen rain, while barges on their
final journey for the season navigate her arteries,
pushing waves through intricate backwater veins.

> *Oh, Mighty Mississippi!*

I drive alone, but suddenly Ananya and Dipankar are
here in my mind aboard this journey. I'm not sure
why you two are here. Of all people, why you two

To be riding with me up the mighty river highway
on this damp, blustery day? This is not your landscape
or climate. You are tropical city dwellers.

Why are you here?
 Where is Meena? Where's Srija?

There is something in these trees,
this highway of concrete,
a path that leads, both sides
of this road are calling me.

This dancing breeze, November's
whistling wind pushes waves across
highway lines as I steer towards
returning to you.

But here you are,
Ananya in the backseat, Dipankar in the front,
talking endless and passionate.
You have lifetimes to talk about
and always will,

Dipankar facing sideways, finger pointing,
Diva of the backseat topping every point,
Exclamations reigning everywhere,
The conversation will never finish,
Never!

You two are brother and sister in my mind
And like brothers and sisters, love and bicker.

I smile silent,
Keep my rock'n roll down low
and the windows rolled up with the heat on high
though I'd rather relish a fresh blast of outside air,
moist and cold and true.

I'm wondering if your conversation will pause
and you will notice these trees calling to me.

Do you see that the out-of-the-way trails through
these valleys are in my veins?

Silently, I shift the car to a lower gear, wondering
why this route suddenly seems so profound
when nothing has been for a while.

I believe in feeling, but I don't feel it.
I feel believing but can't see it.

Can't stomach the gravity and don't like to argue
with voices jostling vigorously as I ponder
what we will leave behind and why will we leave it?

Endless injustice. What to do with the anger?
Turmoil strikes rage in the purest of hearts.
Wasteful endeavors make folly of truths that don't add up.

Would you blow yourself up?
Make the ultimate sacrifice?
For statement? For cause?
For a way out?
For the family?
For history?

Will the world evolve by our anger matching
the injustice of the world?

It would be jingoist of me to answer.
A white man's privilege can hardly penetrate
the indecency of entitlement, generations of abuse,

traveling not this familiar road through enticing
forests in my skin but driving through Texas and
fearing for life, driven off the road for terrorist skin,
pulled over for being minor in the eyes of a major,
followed by suspicious clerks in department stores,
placed in a jail cell for a misdemeanor,
        a weight so heavy it leads to hanging.

How could I know discrimination?

How will I understand the resentment
of generations, religion banished,
language succumbed to a foreign tongue?

Antiquities of a growing world.
What to do with the anger, the endless
discrimination? To know my foe as my sister,
how she perceives, what makes her grow —

Why think they the way they do?
What do they really think of you?

Have they drank too much at weddings?
Felt slighted by a ruse? Do we all seek
love above endeavors?

What would *"we"* like to do to *"them?"*
Blow up their shopping malls? Gouge out
their eyes?

Deprive communities of future brilliance?
Create alternatives for a future to evolve?
Why do we fight ourselves? How are we
our own worst enemy?

How can I speak to such resentment?
Understand such rage? Bear witness to
devastation of slavery and colonization?
Comprehend the hatred flowing through
ethnic cleansing and cultural appropriation?

Our time is short.
Isn't it all about sharing
what we've got, what we know,
      what we feel and what we hope?

You say we're not all in this together.
You are color, I am not.

This is very difficult.

For you, for me.
Are we not brothers and sisters?

Trite idealistic nonsense, you say,
Protestant malarkey unmindful
of deep ramifications contained herein.

Hippies with hearts on high,
stoned in privileged relevancy,
outraging villagers in Thailand
      with nude dances on sacred shores,
brochures for purchased culture,
graffiti on temples, transparent
ignorance of grace,

Hippies with our hearts on high,
holding signs outside the boardroom,
never to relate, to ever stop the hate and
heckling, seldom crossing
that border but to sell.

Gone and dead, we all will soon be.
I feel it on this dark November.
I feel the silence blowing out our
words when thoughts are done.

Your conversation has ended and
now I'm alone again in the car,
knowing soon my car and I will
no longer travel this road.

The forsaken arteries lurk in the
darkness behind me for others.

Waves may consume the highway,
but some path will lead on.

Glass Hockey Stick

Still drunk on a badly ended affair,
lurking shamed and private
in shadows of recess,

eloquently spinning on banana peels for those
betting on the races, trampling tulips, peeing in
the sandlot, demigods and gargoyles,
fed up with anecdotes treading in the limelight of
acceptance.

Now off,
into the fervor of a lifeline,
       denying access to tomorrow,
defying wisdom of ancestors randomly tossed
to the clicking of a turnstile, knocked out of step
by a smartphone text triggering emotion.

Nervous laughter surrenders to the dizzying
environment in a subway tunnel with little
hope of escape should terrorists seize
the next train or police club the minority.

Staggering on high heels, trying to get
attention just to slap it, hoping someone
breaks through the craziness to stay up
late with in old age, insuring passion

is not just for the young and cynicism
is only passing the puck across the ice
toward another goal.

The Indiscretion of Solitude

I.

Temptress on the precipice
of reasoning.

Tough issues of privilege and race
slam hope and ideals in protest
of retribution, fueled by jealousy
and frustration.

>Angry rebellion on a day to garden –
>   weeding, planting,
>   pruning, digging,
>   manufacturing dew.

>>*Where grow I?*

Longing
for the discretion of solitude,
sitting in a windowsill, pondering
life's complexities in hounding
motion to the body, to the mind,
difficult conundrum of reality,
heated to boil, then cool.
Short flame blown to the wind.

True deep hues of being survive, adapting
to university errors, a conductor's lapse,
a tempo hurried, stolen breaths from history's
execution of bakers'n mothers'n brothers'n friends,
whales'n oceans and forests endangered,
bombs reigning down turning giggles to rubble,
doughnut hole drains the suburban thick frosting
holding us together with the TV in 3D. Reality,
why do you taunt me so?

Arrogant and greedy, where go I?
Who has stolen, lied and compromised
What I thought right for my own awkward might,
Weeding leaders to let weak flowers grow.

Timid and pale in the morning light, able
to roust a pup's soul with a promise of adventure.
Discarding molds of tenacious belonging
and seeking forth true
conviction of dew.

II.

Are there any words that need to be faced?
Really need to be said?

Any new core to explore
on a snow-blind afternoon looking forward and back?

Winds blow and ghosts come visit.
How weary I've become of the world
    grown larger and smaller,

Reaching that age where I believe nothing,
suspect everything, and am overwhelmed
by most of it.

Tourist bombs, beheaded hosts,
striving towards destinations
disastrously expensive.
      There'll be no resources for the future
unless the ammunition feeds.

The love we make unequal
to the wake of our indifference
towards enemies and neighbors,
an overcrowded raft weighed down,
barely afloat as glaciers crash into
rising oceans of biblical prophecy,
rising upwards like an angry dog
under armed, nuclear clouds.

 On most channels, you can still get reruns from
      the seventies, access to fuel adolescent dreams
as long as credit holds.

Where do all the dead cellphones go? Can't I just
fix this thing instead of adding to the junk pile?

Technology obsolete before the cows come home.
Prescription changed, path upgraded
as we grandfathers'n babies struggle and stride
to live and share our blood stories.

I've no solutions any more.
Just my own contentions to refine,
cutting down waste and irrelevance.

Raising a tadpole
in a cesspool tide, swirling,
trying to gage the magnanimity of the landscape
while scrambling with the flush,

I'm not intrigued with trinkets
nor sentiments of dreams so
high they desecrate the ground.

Tired,
wanting a shady chair to catch the breeze from.
Not really that old but
worn out.

Fire drill over, bake sale proceeds spent.
There is little time
to collect dimes and forget the rhymes.

Winds subside
and ghosts vacate.

They say, admitting your mistakes
is the closest thing to innocence.

Glowing embers retreating,
I wonder,
cautiously aghast,
of it all too much.

III.

Discrete breeze awakens
fresh, unloved,
subsided by divine intervention and karmic
comeuppance. A miracle of reckoning!

as I stir to Big Sur days, at home, at peace,
inside and out, no need
for policing which only arms hatred,
dividing humans into enemies.

I cannot live in a world of shadows.
As strange as it may be, the truth
must be released.

No walking a plank of narrow living.
Uncloak the soldier, see the man.
Let it all out, bare the test.

Unveil the soul -- the heart, those dreams.
Don't wanna die with any secrets, drowned
in concealed passion. Don't wanna
live without living, die without
dying, scream without screaming, love
without loving.

To lie in the spray of a rainbow's waterfall,
wedged in the sand, water rushing over
the rocks and across my skin, letting
goosebumps tickle my soul,

Old and still yet young, feeling
the felonies of generations, retribution,
crimes of passion, burdens of failed
dreams, all wash over me — nightmares
of reasonable demise put to the
test, cowering unafraid,

to balance on towering
cliffs of imperfect dignity
with ample pressure pushing
my pride over the edge
to balance *my true soul.*

Where beyond this bliss go I?
Into what? With whom? To
hallways of mortal certainty?

Astute to a darkness enveloping,
where many won't go, spectators don't glimpse
gathering televised truths with populist blessings,

pleading for love and
sanity with a cold bullet
pointed homeward,

as I awake to Big Sur days,
inalienable, at peace.

Twilight

Translucent smiles of affection
won't let false hope succeed
to hold a tiny, warm hand across
a cold November street

from an orphanage unfunded
to pillars of mistrust and fear.

With as much love as human error will allow,
the consequence of confusion, the pain of logic
eats away all hunger in my brain

as that tiny hand
remains, clutching
Don't let love go astray,

holding firm
onto a brilliant twilight
simmering with fascination
on the horizon.

Limboland

Gonna lay my aching soul out
on a flatbed truck tonight,
   fading out to stars above Montana
as the highway rumbles beneath
   and the longnecks swish inside.

Wishing I hadn't mislaid my pride,
dancing at the inauguration ahead of the tide
with rustlers hustling doodads and hip fads
who faded like thirty-foot high movie screens into worn
blue jeans,
past screams of teens whistling limelight on the moor,
acting fast on a walnut, washed down
in a stream of old apartments, window broken,
wind beating in, stairway creaking of ghosts
on a cold November morning, frozen.

Waking, shivering to the dawn.
Trying to remember how we ever got along, distancing
ourselves from the true realms of dreams,
rebating possibilities, rejecting cautious cures

as dusty moonlit gamblers lay their soiled cards down
to dance with the arrangers of insignificance,
sanctifying whims of a suffering path evolutionary
towards perpetual dusk.

While I, on hand at dawn
for the cold morning chill in the recruitment of
believers, wince

at the blinding, heated light of dancers
in the distance, a mighty resonance of love
that isn't lost on the rhythms of iron engineers
rusting their arms on the mirage
of a conflict-free existence in a paycheck.

After all is said and done,
      is loss lost, are winnings won?

Love, hated and humiliated, wades
    in a murky, misdirected shipwreck
without a guide through history's abuse
as bloodshed ailing millions doesn't stain the oiled
machine,
blasting earth into worn craters, frozen deserts,
sterile forests, radioactive moms.

      We smile, cancerous,
              our neon emblems blazing
in the unforgiving night.

I've a long way to go before I leave this world
a little better than I found it,
      sustainable with a little human growth,
heat from our loving with tools from our trades,
uncovering the formation of our future with
abundance from the sun, wind and rising oceans.

We've a long way to go
to get over the hump of terror.
White knuckled chandeliers wagging carrots
in front of carts,
beefing up brilliance as though it never existed,
sniffing up angel dust with a confident grimace,
guarding a back wallet with a gyrating groin.
Misfits emptied of character. Dervishes steadfast.
Coins collected from a fountain of wishes.
Beauty and death. Lingering unrest.

Should Earth hurl itself suddenly
into the sun, heated from within,
imploding, shaken to nothingness,

would still our songs echo through
the universe like fields of sunflowers
blazing in the night?

There's danger in each stroke.
The pain of transience
in the divinity of infinity.

Gonna lay my aching soul
out on a flatbed truck tonight,
fading out to stars above Montana,
stars so close they pull you to eternity,

smiling, knowing,
even a heartbreak
is better than naught.

www.ingramcontent.com/pod-product-compliance
Lightning Source LLC
Chambersburg PA
CBHW030448300426
44112CB00009B/1214